I think that an ideal introduction to this book ca previous volume on the same area but written Dolling entitled 'Ten Years in a Portsmouth S

GW00370631

"In earlier days Charlotte Street was of the number of butchers shops behind it. It was a main thoroughfa to and from their place of work. Local streets were often named after sea admirals and their battles; houses with old red tiled roofs and tiny rooms like ships cabins. The scent of the sea mixed where, courting, fighting, drinking and laughing; all mingling in this poor little district with its 1,100 houses and 52 pubs.

The street itself was an open fair from one end to the other with cheap-jacks screaming their wares, laughing crowds around them but never actually seeming to buy anything, women haggling with vendors and trying to get their Sunday dinners a bit cheaper because things had started to go a bit stale."

This then was the picture painted by the well known and respected local priest when he first came to the area over 100 years ago when utter poverty was the way of life for most inhabitants.

Most things have improved a lot over the passing years but I think a lot of the above can still be seen albeit having changed a bit with the times. To me the biggest change must be the virtual absence of our Naval friends, but I dare say a lot of our older readers will carry vivid memories of them in the street.

Although titled Charlotte Street, the reader will find that, unlike the first edition (printed in 1987) this version does not confine itself just to that thoroughfare but ventures into the many side streets and alleys that made up this colourful area.

Some other memories of the area date back even further still, in the 1920s William Tarring wrote his memories of the area. He was born in 1840 and writes of a time when the area was hardly developed.

"Clarence Street at that time bore quite a rural aspect, on the west side were allotments and market gardens. At the top was a meadow often with horses grazing, and backed by an open outlook of gardens. On the east side a narrow road, Bowley's Lane, led to cowsheds and dairy premises with a small meadow beyond, where I used to play, the whole of which has long been included in the

1

hospital grounds. Next to this was a large room known as the 'Bell School' for boys a gaunt bare, miserable room with a stone floor cold and desolate so unlike the present palatial style of school buildings.

The public roads in early days were under the jurisdiction of the 'Highways Board' who were not very painstaking. There was no paved channelling but in winter miniature ditches. The road was mended with pebbly gravel, left to be ground down by the ordinary traffic of the district, producing mud in winter and dust in Summer. Our water supply was perhaps our brightest feature, nearly all the houses had a well, but water for drinking purposes was supplied at a farthing a bucket from a horse-drawn cask. The said water being pumped from one of several springs in the neighbourhood. My father had a parrot who was greatly interested in the transactions. When after a time the cart ceased its visits, 'Poll' transferred her interest to the milkman, and as soon as she heard the sound of the milk can, used to explain 'Here's the Water'."

Charlotte Street was built in line with the strips of one of the furlongs of the old West Dock Field. A few buildings are shown on maps dating back as far back as 1773. The western portion was originally called George Street, after King George and later was known as New Charlotte Street. The eastern portion was Bloody Row, named due to the number of butchers and slaughterhouses. The whole street was renamed Charlotte Street after the wife of King George the third.

General Memories

My Aunt was born in Clarence Street at the turn of the century and lived there till about 1916. For the next few years she lived in Cornwall but by about 1920 she was back in the city where she spent the rest of her life. Her memory always seemed to be quite remarkable from her early schooldays until her demise in the early 1990s.

> "Our house in Clarence Street was no different to any of the other in the area - small. Its only claim to fame was that it was next door neighbour was Father Dolling. He was remembered by my sisters and me as a kindly man who raised no objections to us children making mud pies on his doorstep. His usual comment was "Oh dear, I will have to get my housekeeper to clean it off." I don't know what her comment was. My school was Conway Street and

my younger sister and myself would go either to Thomas Street and down to school or the other way through Charlotte Street. The latter was much more interesting with all the shops and the people."

She then mentioned what it was like walking down Charlotte Street on the right hand side from the Commercial Road end and back up the other. Unfortunately I do not know whether this was pre World War 1 when she lived there or between the wars when she would have shopped there.

"On the corner of Charlotte Street was a sports hall with cinema, boxing facilities etc. Then came Davidson's clothes. On the corner of Pye Street was an office for Dittman & Malpas or Curtis. These were followed by a couple of small shops. Then Landport Street. Kitters the Jewish dress shop, the Portsmouth Arms and Clarence Street. Brooks the grocers followed by a picture frame shop and Jerams fruit, veg and flower shop. Then came Chance Street with Jones' shellfish shop on the corner. An oddment shop was Mack's. Then came Hope Street and Georges the leather shop. Slapes wet and dried fish, a pet shop selling all kinds of pet food was Paynes. Then came Amelia Street the Golden Bell, Kellaways pawn shop, a small music shop, a narrow path leading to St. Agathas then Conway Street. With the Welcome Restaurant with a Mission Hall above."

For some reason she never went on down to Unicorn Road but crossed Charlotte Street to Cox's Hotel and Little Charlotte Street

"With its old hat shop. Coming back towards Commercial Road was a cake and bread shop called Vallers, Smith's sweet shop and a second hand shop. Augusts selling papers and cigarettes and Jacks old fashioned sweet shop. On the corner of Meadow Street was a chemists and on the opposite corner was a very old rummage shop - Lamkins, Busseys the pork butchers, Arnetts fish shop, a small grocers and another small shop which I believe was Lloyds surgical equipment. A butchers shop, Smiths the egg and poultry merchants, Gassers butchers shop, a small trinket and jewellery shop and finally on the corner of Commercial Road was Shipps the fruiterer. Moores Square about half way down with 2 or 3 old houses in an alley. On the corner was Rosies shop selling groceries and allsorts."

Nell Gray

3

Charlotte Street is without doubt one of the most memorable and nostalgic of all Portsmouth thoroughfares since the turn of the century. Running from Commercial Road to Unicorn Road it consisted of numerous shops and stalls, that catered for almost every commodity required by the average household. It was a regular weekend venue for families to visit, where for a few pence comics and sweets would content the children, whilst the various traders sometimes "sold off" their goods at almost give-a-way prices as closing time of the market approached. Most of the traders handed down their businesses to their next of kin, therefore many of the same names still exist, giving good value and service to the public, as in the days of their parents. Apart from these genuine people there were also a number of cheap jacks who often frequented the street offering various wares to the sometimes gullible public in search of a "bargain". They employed various ruses to attract attention around their stalls, many of which can still be remembered by older Portsmouthians. Unfortunately the street and its surroundings suffered considerable damage during World War II, consequently very few of the original buildings remained and those that did were demolished to make way for the Cascades Shopping Centre.

Therefore with the help of a few contributors and a Kelly's directory we endeavour to take our readers back approximately fifty years, with a view to reviving a few memories of yesteryear. It should be noted that some shops changed hands frequently so they may not appear exactly as you recall.

"On a Saturday all the shops and stalls were opened 'til 9 o'clock, the shop inspectors used to be in the street to see you did close on time. Christmas times were busy times, but a very happy atmosphere was felt throughout the street. As a boy I remember the flare lights on the stalls, the cheap jacks would throw china on the floor if no one bought the goods. "Gold" watches sold for £1 and pills and ointments to cure all ailments were also sold by the cheap jacks. On Saturday night it was almost impossible to walk through the street it was so packed with people. When the people had gone home the barrow boys used to tip what was left of the fruit and veg in the road and along came the scavengers to see what they could find. After a while the street cleaners came and swept the road, and on a Sunday morning they came round and washed the road. Christmas time when I was a boy the butchers at the end of the day would almost give the meat away, it was fun to watch the traders."

Back in the twenties it really was Charlotte Street, with the market and traders, who were mostly called costers. In the old days it was an education to walk

4

through Charlotte Street market, as far as I know it was a chartered market. The traders used to pull their barrows out from Fridays at 1pm and all days Saturdays. My mother and father had their pitches in the Unicorn Road Market and I remember now how I used to be up at 4am to get down to the market with an orange box and sit there until my father came down from the wholesale market which was held in Commercial Road. Otherwise someone else would be in there and in those days we paid nothing for our stalls to stand there and could stay out sometimes 'til 10 or 11pm until we sold out. There used to be buskers, bards and different entertainers all day and what talent you could see, it was as good as going to the theatre. There used to be quite a number of pubs in the street and I can see the police and the navy patrol every Friday and Saturday night after the pubs shut patrolling up and down to stop any trouble and how the navy patrol used to what we knew as 'Frog March' them back to barracks if they caused any trouble. The costers who sold their fruit and veg always helped each other in those days, and the arguments were settled on a Sunday mornings round what was called the mews, a big stable yard for horses, cows and sheep and how I used to run down there to see them settle their arguments as many as six bare fist fights. But after it was settled they bore no malice, they would shake hands and go for a drink in the pub on the corner, the Charlotte Street Cellars, later nicknamed the speak-easy. I can see Charlotte Street now at night weekends when it was dark in the winter with the old paraffin flare lamps hung up over the stall, as it didn't start really busy 'til about 6pm. There was also a union called the Coster Mongers Union which was held at the Empire Pub in Somers Road North where some of the traders used to hold a leg of mutton supper every so often for 6d each, the union fee was 3d a week. Of course the market was hard hit during the war, as the traders were not allowed to stand there with their wares owing to the black out. It is not the street it used to be in pre-war days as it is controlled by the council now, and trading has been restricted and the large shops are out-trading the small traders in the street, but I hope there will always be a Charlotte Street market as the tradition has been handed down from families generation to generation. I've been to other town's markets and to me Charlotte Street market is the best and cheapest market I've yet to see."

"In the thirties, my parents and I, would walk from Fawcett Road to Charlotte Street, carrying our straw shopping bags to bring back the weekend groceries. If it was wet, out came my Woolies wellies. If it was cold then I wore stout boots cobbled by my father, with plenty of hob-nails and to keep my legs warm, I had soft leather gaiters which buttoned up the side. My father often wore stiff leather leggings which were kept on with straps, together with ex-army riding breeches, and my mother would often put brown wrapping paper under my shirt and in my boots. I'm sure all this helped to keep me warm. On arrival at the market we would start at one end, usually Commercial Road end, and work our way along the very crowded street, buying a bit from one barrow and then some more veg from another. I'm sure my mother had her favourite barrow boys which she preferred to buy from, for we always seemed to stop in the same places. Mother did the buying, we were the porters. One barrow boy that sticks in my mind, is the one that sold peanuts. His barrow was piled high with them, and he would call out "Tuppence a pint, penny 'alf pint, peanuts". His pitch was one of the first barrows you saw as you went into the street. If we had to wait for mother to be served or while she was making up her mind, I would sometimes play with other children. One of the games we would do would be to race match boxes up and down in the rain filled gutter. Further down the street I used to play with the puppies and kittens which were in cages. They looked so pathetic, and seemed to almost ask you to buy them and give them a good home, but when I asked my parents if I could have one, I always got the same reply, a very firm NO, but as compensation they would buy me some home made boiled sweets from Jacks, and with any luck a 1d bundle of American comics. My father would call in at George's to buy pieces of leather and nails, and next door, he would examine the display of working clothes in Jordans, possibly buying the odd Union shirt, which was warm and hard wearing. I can remember seeing the Navy square rigged flannel shirts on sale there, they had a square neck with a blue band around the edge. By this time, our shopping bags were getting full, and if it was raining, it was very difficult to keep my roll of comics dry. Many a time I had to spread them out on our iron fender in front of the fire to dry them out, before I could read them. We gradually moved through the throng of people, stopping to hear the spiel, traders selling bed sheets, pillowcases, etc.. The calls of the barrow boys could be heard ringing out the full length of the street, with the flare lamps hanging above their wares, hissing and casting their glow over the street scene. Finally it was decided to make our way home and leave the noise and bustle of Charlotte Street for the comparative peace of Commercial Road. Making our way to the Guildhall Square to catch the tram in Greetham Street."

Frank Ford

"A great shopping market known for miles in the south and the Isle of Wight. The cash flow must have been terrific. Stalls and shops all good value and quality as well. People came from Southampton and the Isle of Wight on

Saturdays mostly and say that the visit to the market paid for their journey, so reasonable and good. I remember back before the First World War the bright blue arc lamps illuminating the merchandise, especially the turkey display at Christmas, hundreds hanging outside the shops. In those days of no refrigerators and if the weather suddenly became warmer the prices of turkeys and poultry dropped with a bang! The stalls had the proprietors names above them and a good standard was usually maintained. The acetylene illuminations also giving a weird glow. The tradesmen were certainly characters, and were part of and blended with the environment and deserved every penny of what they made, especially being out in the open in winter, in the rain and cold. To walk along Charlotte Street on Christmas Eve was a fascinating journey, noise and clatter, hundreds and hundreds of people jostling for the last minute bargains, Christmas trees, turkeys etc., everyone talking, the stall holders shouting at the top of their voices extolling the goodness and cheapness of their wares. All classes and types mingled, after all who doesn't want a bargain, especially a good one."

"When the ice wagon arrived in the area to deliver the blocks of ice to the fishmongers and butchers, the children would quickly gather. As the driver drove his steel hook into the block of ice, to drag it nearer to the edge of the wagon, slivers of ice would splinter off and the children would scramble to pick up these pieces, and stand around gleefully sucking them before they melted. I suppose this must have been the fore-runner of the ice-lolly. The Iceman as we called him was a familiar sight in our young days, humping the block of ice on his shoulder, which was covered by sacks. I suppose this helped to prevent it melting before he had a chance to deliver it. He must have had to move fairly fast in the summer."

"I lived in Lake Road quite near to Charlotte Street for thirty four years and as a child we used to go to Charlotte Street on Saturdays and spend hours and hours down there. There were lots of little streets in the area and each had its own character. During the war in 1941, I had moved to Fratton, and on this night I think it was Christmas Eve, we heard a terrible roaring like thousands of rattles going and we could hear all the way from Charlotte Street to Fratton. I worked on the Corporation and the following day we were sent down and I have never seen anything like it in my life, because there were whole streets with the roofs hanging off houses, and at the end of one road, the junction of Copenhagen, Conway and Chalton Streets, was a huge crater, it must have been at least fifteen to twenty feet deep covering the whole of the road. If it was a bomb, we don't know even now, it may have been a plane, it was never broadcast and we were sent there to find anything appertaining to a bomb and we found nothing. Just bricks and stuff. Before the war there were all small shops from one end to another of Charlotte Street, greengrocers, faggots and pease pudding shops, whelk shops and everything you could think of.

On the corner outside Shipps was a round kiosk and they sold cheap cigarettes and tobacco, they used to do quite a trade. On the corner of Spring Street when I was a child used to be a man with ropes and chains and he used to ask people in the audience to tie him up. One Saturday when he said "I guarantee to get out of these chains in about four or five minutes if anyone will tie me up". Some sailors tied him up and put a sack over his head and tied some string around it The poor bounder, he had said he would give five shillings to anyone who could keep him there, they let him go for five to ten minutes and in the end he was laying on the ground struggling. Of course they had to untie him, so they got his five shillings.

The store holders had beautiful trucks and barrows, painted in brilliant colours, reds, blues and greens and the carts drawn by ponies had a headboard at the front painted with their names in beautiful colours. There was an article in the paper about a fire at Stanley's store, where they stored a lot of trucks and barrows, they have been there for years and all this stuff has been burnt. It's really the biggest loss for that kind of thing, even now I can see weddings with some of these trucks with the Bride and Groom sitting up with the driver, Mr. Stanley used to hire them out. As children we used to live on pecked fruit, the stall holders weren't allowed to sell anything that had gone off, so what they used to do was throw it in an old orange box laying on the ground and we children used to fold up our jersey and fill it with apples and pears and oranges, go around the corner, cut off the bad bits and eat the rest. Well I have lived to quite a ripe old age now so they never hurt me at all."

Dave Jenkins

"My earliest recollections of Charlotte Street, were when I was a very young child, were all the small shops that ran from Commercial Road practically the whole length of Charlotte Street. There was an extraordinary number, at least it seemed to me then as a child. These small shops were kept by immigrants, which I believe from information I have gathered since were Polish and Russian Jews, who came here before and during the First World War. They had unpronounceable names but took new names when they became naturalised citizens. On Saturdays the market was packed and it must have been after nine when the stalls packed up. The street used to be literally knee deep in rubbish from the stalls, the council workman started at about ten o'clock and went through Charlotte Street and every bit would be cleared up. And then on Sunday morning they used to wash the street from end to end, starting at around seven o'clock in the morning. They had a water cart and using brooms and disinfectant they would start at Commercial Road end and work their way through to the end, and I guarantee that Charlotte Street in those days was cleaner than any road I've seen anywhere."

"There was an elderly man who used to stroll through the market with a neck tray containing bags of cough sweets. As he walked he'd be calling out "Paregoric cough no more". On normal weekdays his stand was outside the Dockyard Unicorn Gate."

"Saturday night and on to Charlotte Street market. The atmosphere was superb, the whole street was lit with naphthalene flares all giving out a guttering fitful light and hissing menacingly in the wind. These flares were fantastic in the chill winter weather and seemed to lend a cheerful air to the hustle and bustle and the raucous cries of the traders touting their wares. Kippers by the dozen, magic mixtures to cure grannies direst cough, the shell fish shop with live winkles trying to escape back to those bleak tidelands by climbing up the plate glass windows, vying with fat whelks to reach safety before the next customer abducted them to unwanted waters and a far hotter reception. Puppies, kittens and rabbits in cages waiting for new owners kind or otherwise, wild birds fluttering wildly at the cruel wires, desperately seeking the freedom of the countryside, a greenfinch cost 6d whilst a cock Goldfinch cost half a crown."

"On the Monday morning, after the bombing raid of Jan 10th 1941, I left my home at Cosham, very early on my bike and found the road to the city centre was open. Moreover it was lined on both sides by large lorries full of fruit and vegetables. I asked a bystander what was going on? "Why our market of course". The morning market was usually held in Charlotte Street but that was still burning, so they had settled on this stretch of road to do their business. I went sometimes to pedal along roads that looked untouched; and sometimes having to push my bike carefully among the broken glass along the roads that had been so badly burnt or blasted that I could hardly recognise where I was. I picked my way along the remains of Charlotte Street, some of the buildings were still smouldering and one wall fell down suddenly in my path. It crossed my mind whether Charlotte Street would ever look the same again. My destination was the college where I was due to take an exam, from my desk near the window, I could see the Guildhall itself with the crooked cupola. I started wondering if it was going to fall on me, to my stressed mind it seemed to be swaying at every breath of the wind. Looking back on it later on, I think this was just the effect of the cold air on the still very hot metal."

"During the past decades, many senior citizens have noted several changes in Charlotte Street. From the naphthalene lamps to the modern lighting arrangements of today brings back many memories of yesteryear. The section towards Spring Street was usually occupied by here today gone tomorrow cheapjacks who sold some useful and some useless to the gullible public. These salesmen were a class of their own and were often accompanied by assistants who drew a crowd by chewing razor blades, offering to be tied up, having flagstones broken on their chests, swallowing lighted fire tapers and many other ruses. All to the great amusement of we youngsters who disappeared when the hat was passed around."

"I liked the trips I took with Mum to Charlotte Street. There were cages with chickens and rabbits, if you wanted one they would kill it on the spot. In those days you knew it was fresh! These days everything is frozen until the taste has gone out of it. There was a man with a covered wagon on which was painted "Dentist Painless Extraction". People went inside thinking it won't hurt me. Once inside however, the dentist would employ a man with a drum and a trumpet to drown the screams of the victim! Another instance concerned the Salvation Army. Someone had died abroad and his body had been brought back home. The Salvation Army had him embalmed and put him on show in Charlotte Street. I remember my mother and brother saying it was a pity to put him underground as he only looked to be sleeping! It turned out that the chap was my friend Nora's brother"

Vera Sparkes

Charlotte Street Point Duty

"This point was worked from 9am to 5pm with a relief, usually from 12.30 to 1.30pm by the relief man on the beat. The point was a very busy one, more busy at the weekend of course, as the point was on the main road. The market traders used to bring their barrows across from Paradise Street to Charlotte Street, to set them up for the day, and of course you helped them as much as you could. The point also controlled a pedestrian crossing. The point is no longer worked and the old buildings in the vicinity have disappeared although many of the names of the traders have been passed down. Names that come to mind are Warwicks, Wearns, Deacons and Webb. Mr. Webb is still in the market. We never got any trouble from the traders, they seemed to sort their own troubles and it was left at that. We had to work in all weathers and we were supplied with white waterproof coats and leggings. We also had our own additions to keep the warmth in or cold out, personally I wore an army leather jerkin, which I found very satisfactory. Outside the Emperor of India pub was a blue painted Police Box, this was used by me and the beat man if we wanted to get in touch with the station, in those days we were not equipped with personal radios. Although the point was very busy, I cannot remember any unpleasant incidents of any type in the eighteen months I was on the point. I have been asked did it make my arms ache? Well at first it did, but after a while I got used to it."

Portsmouth Street Traders Association 1895

They had a colourful banner, which was made by George Tuthill Ltd. in 1896. On one side it depicted a street scene of the vegetable market in Commercial Road, with horse drawn wagons lined up on each side of the road and a donkey drawn barrow loaded with vegetables making its way along the road, being led by the trader. The stretch of road it shows is between Crasswell Street and Lake Road. Buildings shown are Porter Bros, Mortons Boots, The Duke of York, the Prince of Wales and the Gaiety Theatre. A turn of the century view it also bears the motto on this side "Defence not Defiance"

On the reverse the picture is of the Guildhall as a backdrop (known as the Townhall in those days). It shows a trader whose loaded barrow has lost a wheel and has tipped the produce in the path of an oncoming horse drawn tram. A second trader has stopped and is offering to lend a hand. A local bobby is surveying the scene, with a crowd that has gathered. Along the top edge of this side is "We claim the right to live" and along the bottom edge is written "United we stand, divided we fall"

The association was wound up in 1972

Typical Street Scene in the 50s

M.S.G. 1994

By piecing together lists from several contributors we have arrived at the following list of stalls commencing from Commercial Road

>Shipps - Fruit & Veg
>>Sold from the open fronted shop
>
>Three Women or an elderly couple - Flowers
>>"Mr. and Mrs. Jones would set out early to the railway station and collect boxes of flowers from Petersfield, Wickham and Winchester. When they got back to the market on a small hand cart they were sorted and placed in banks on old boxes and planks in buckets and bowls filled with water. You could get a large and varied bunch for 1/6d (7.5p). Sometimes when winter set in and near Christmas they had Holly Wreaths they made, they also sold paper and waxed flowers but not often as there was nearly always something in season."
>
>Elderly Man & Women - Peanuts
>>In season they sold watercress at a 1d a bunch.
>
>Date Stall
>>Large blocks of dates 4d a pound, they were un-stoned.
>
>Bell - fishmonger
>
>Clarks - Bananas
>>Still there.
>
>Garcia - The Chocolate King
>
>Onion Stall
>>Sold only onions
>
>George Smith - tame rabbits
>
>Gasser - butcher
>
>Arnett - fishmonger
>>This is the family that now run the Crown Bingo and Amusement Machine Arcades.
>
>Lamkin - fruit & Veg
>
>Webbs - Puppies & Kittens
>
>Marsh - fruiterer
>
>Steele, Fancy Goods & Toys
>
>Valvona - fruiterer
>
>August - newsagent
>
>Old Jacks - boiled sweets
>>Large variety at 4d a pound
>
>Bryants - newsagent

Davidson - clothes
Gaiman - grocer
Cough - Candyman
China Stall

> "Tea sets could be bought from around 3/6d (17.5p). The man used to pile up a whole tea set very systematically on one hand, toss it up and catch it. He was most entertaining with his patter and always had an audience."

> "He stood on a makeshift rostrum amongst his wares. Pottery seconds he sold. He would stand there and lead forth with a voice like a foghorn. "Oi! - come on who'll give me a shilling, no, not a shilling - a tanner? two dinner plates. Right Bob lady over there." His assistant takes them to the women who proffers two shillings. The China King looks up and says "I say lady four plates, two cups and saucers all for your two bob". She is delighted as they are quickly wrapped up. He was a blessing to young married couples who were setting up their first homes, an eighteen or twenty one piece tea set 5/6d and perhaps a babies chamber pot thrown in for fun, he was always on cue and knew any newly weds."

Italian

> "During the winter he would always be there with his stall selling roast chestnuts or baked potatoes. In summer he would be there with his ice-cream barrow, cornets and wafers, ½d and 1d each. In the evenings he was at the theatre queues."

Pascoes - fishmongers

> "I remember Mr. Pascoe holding up quite a large smoked haddock for a tanner. And have heard him say if trade seemed slow "What's the matter with you all? A tanner for this large haddock, who'll give me a bob for two?" Funnily enough they would then sell like hot cakes."

Other stalls we have not placed were fruiterers Stanleys, Deacons, Porters, Treagus, Wakes and Wheatcroft; Herbalist Green, Greengrocers Killiford and Warren.

We commence our look in detail on the south side and at the junction with Commercial Road

3   **George Shipp**, Potato Merchant

If the numbering has remained the same over the years this was in 1887 the Peoples Coffee Tavern. Shipps now have a shop around the corner in Meadow Street (1987).

"A big shop with stalls outside. They would sell all kinds of fresh vegetables, they were renowned potato salesmen I remember Mrs. Shipp, also her two daughters that used to sell produce in the shop whilst the father and sons sold and supplied the stall outside. The fruit was always plentiful and trade was very fast indeed, they never called their wares out like smaller traders would have to."

5 **Dick's Boot Stores**
"In Dick's I used to buy very high heeled black velvet shoes with ankle straps 4/11d a pair, I was about 16 or 17 then."

7A **John Farmer Ltd**, Boot and Shoe Dealers
9 **Herbert Bell**, Fishmonger
11 **Harvey Sheinning**, Clothier
13 **H. Thomas (B.W.Parsons Ltd)**, Butcher
15 **Joseph McMaster,** Butcher
17 **Robert Pikesley**, Greengrocer
19 **Arthur Taplin,** Butcher

Was previously Daniel Garcia, The Chocolate King" who moved to Commercial Road.

"He would have large slabs of chocolate, milk, dark or Brazil nut, very thick and broken up by toffee hammers. He also sold boxes of Rowntrees chocolates 2/- a pound box and Frys bars as well as loose chocolates with no makers name but still good enough at 1/- a pound. At Easter and Christmas he would sell the usual novelties, Easter Eggs and chocolate tree decorations."

"Good quality brand chocolates mostly sold with a continuous patter .... not 10/-, not 7/6d, not 6/-, not 3/-, but here you are 2/6d .... and the lot was sold to the enthralled public listening. He must have gone direct to the manufacturers, obtained good discount for cash. The same for cigarettes of all brands, which arrangements suited all concerned."

21 **Mrs. Susan Jeram,** Butcher
23 **The Landport Restaurant**, proprietor William Millam.

"Old Bill's Café, where, early in the morning , you could buy a huge crusty brown roll with beef dripping - delicious."

25	**William Gourd,** Chemist
27-29	**Robert Ware,** Butcher

The Ware family have been in Charlotte Street since 1844 when Robert is listed as a butcher in Pigot's Directory.

"Bob Ware had a farm at Farlington opposite Farlington Church keeping sheep, cows and pigs. He used to have some of the animals taken to Pye Street where the slaughter house was and then he would have meat for his shop"

31 **George Smith,** Poulterer

He was also a bird dealer and pet shop.

"They had a cage for kittens to be sold and always at the end of the day there was more in the cage, reason was the children would come and put their unwanted kittens in the cage when the shop owner wasn't looking."

"Poultry, pet food and canaries. Birds hanging all round the shop."

33-37 **Thomas Gasser,** Butcher

"The veal king of Charlotte Street"

39 **George Cooper,** Pork Butcher

"In the dark days of depression in the early 1930s I had a temporary job for the Christmas period working as a butchers assistant. On Christmas Eve my work for the week was almost at an end, but what an end. At approximately 9pm I was told to clear all the meat on display from the window. Crowds were gathering outside and I was told to go out in front of the shop Then the manager got up into the open window space and started what was to be the clear out sale. He just picked up a joint of meat and offered it, at, to my mind, seemingly cheap prices even for those days. To quote a few prices as I remember them Legs of Lamb 2/6d, Shoulders of Lamb 2/-, Sirloin of Beef 3/-. Then came turkeys, English birds went for 10/- to 12/6d according to weight, then chilled foreign ones 7/6d to 9/-. Lastly frozen birds, these were frozen like blocks of stone, but still people bought them. They sold for 8/- to 10/-. How people thawed them out I cannot say. As all these items were sold my job was to get the meat or bird from the cellar and give it to the customer and collect his or her money. Many times I had trouble with people who claimed they had bought the goods offered, but I could not tell who was right because I was facing the butcher with a massive crowd behind me. Still everything was sorted amicably in the end. It was midnight and I went home happy with my Christmas Box, a beautiful English Turkey."

Charles Hutchins

41   **Mrs. E.A.Hunt,** Pork Butcher

"My father used to tell us of his childhood, like any other boy football was a great love. He played in a team, in later years for St. Agatha's. He and his friends also played in the street and when the French onion man left his cycle outside a pub they tied a piece of black cotton onto the ends of the onion string and when anyone passed they would pull the string and make the onions dance. The onion seller could not work out why they were all moving. My grandfather had people working for him doing the brining of the pork for pickled pork to sell. He kept missing sides of pork and then found out the man who was working for him used to put the sides of meat around his waist and pull his trousers up over them. So one day he kept him talking as he was about to leave, as you can imagine it was cold and icy. The chap could not stand it any longer and had to produce the side of pork and of course he got the sack. My grandfather was said to be able to go to market to select his beasts and could tell by just looking the weight and quality he wanted. On Saturday evenings the gypsies used to come in with their big wicker baskets over their arms. My father used to say to me 2 on 10, I wondered what he meant and was told when ever he said that I was to be alert for it meant two eyes on ten fingers, because they were so quick and would steal bits of meat on the side. My grandmother served in the shop until her death, I remember her as a little old lady dressed in a black dress with lovely jet beads on the front . It was a long dress to the ground covering the black button boots she wore. When she died, I helped in the shop for a while then my mother took over the duties. Someone had to be in the shop while my father was out back cooking the various meats. They worked there until my father sold the shop. He loved that shop and seemed to be there many hours in a day. He was born in the shop. I helped in the shop for a considerable time and knew every nook and cranny of the street. I still have people stop me and say how they miss my father's shop for faggots, tripe, pigs trotters, chitterlings, udder, liver or pigs fry as we knew it."

"Sold hot udder, pigs hocks and feet, also tripe and chitterlings. What a shame the children of today do not know that delicious taste."

"Once a week you queued up for udder 2d."

43	**The People's Prescriptions Ltd.,** Drug Stores
45-47	**Peter Arnett,** Fishmonger

"He had a large store at the rear of the shop in which were kept the banks of fish boxes stacked high. Every type of dry and wet fish you could think of were there, cod, hake, haddock, plaice, soles, dabs, conger eels, and in season mackerel, herrings, sprats. More fish was sold at weekends, the dry fish kept longer and sold well for Sunday breakfasts. He would have a large awning pulled over his shop onto the pavement, with great piles of fish ready to sell cheaply and quickly on Saturday afternoons. He would call out with a loud hoarse voice, "Come on Ma's get yer fish 'ere for breakfast, three large haddock one bob, one bob only, tell yer what'll do put two pairs of kippers and four bloaters ere, 'alf a crown the lot". Which was marvellous value and saved the poor an enormous amount."

"Sold 6d haddock with a handful of sprats for free."

"Dad brought 16 of us up in the fish trade and we all had to work hard, morning to night, and I mean morning 4.30 to 5am. To go over to the fish pound, to get your fish onto the trucks and fetch it back, clean it all, put it in your windows, ready for the Dockyard men at 6.30am and start selling, then you might be at it all day cleaning and serving - you might get an hour for dinner or you might not and you couldn't complain of the cold, because there was nothing wrong with you, for you wasn't sick.

Then we would go curing at night with your bloaters and herrings, and your wages if you were lucky you got eight shillings. I was born in 1918, as there wasn't room for all of us in Charlotte Street, we moved to Abercrombie Street, and I was born in Hanover Street. I never knew what it was to have time off, and if I said to him "Can I have a half day?" he would say "your life is a holiday", mind you he didn't do too much, he just sat back and enjoyed it, but there was nothing that we wanted, when you saw your mates struggling to get something, their wages was nothing, and we got eight bob and that was clear at the time.

My first week I got eight shillings, before leaving school at 14, I also worked, and I might get a shilling for going in on a Friday afternoon, when I was kept home from school for that. He said that once you could read and write, there was no need to go to school, then the war came along, and I did not want to go back to it.

It was too much like hard work, after six years of taking it easy, I did not want to know, no more. Cod used to be tuppence to threepence depending on the size. Plaice was three to four pence a pound, again depending on size. Sprats were tuppence a plate, and I mean a big plate, no argument about it. "If you got no paper you got no B....y fish", that's what we used to tell 'em but they got paper. Halibut was dear at the time, sixpence a pound. Salmon we could buy it in big packages, 400lb packages, in weight, wholesale, on the package was the words "Caught in Pacific Waters 19..." The date could be four years old, and as soon as you received it from the rail, you took it straight out to Mowats Limited, Colpoy Street cold store at the top of Russell Street. It was sold at sixpence ha'penny a pound. Turbot was fourpence a pound. Herrings, we could buy a long hundred, which was a hundred and ten, for a shilling. They sold for a penny each or seven for sixpence, until you got to the big Norway herring which were tuppence each.

When we had done our bloaters, which was done at night, someone had to stay on, to keep the fires burning, you couldn't go to the pictures or anything. Father wouldn't let any of the boys smoke, nor would he let the customers smoke standing over the counter, you never queued in those days you crowded round and we would say "who next" and someone would pipe up "I'm next", perhaps from the back or the front, they all waited their turn.

On a Saturday night you'd have a 'knock-out' get a whole cod, cut it in half, fourpence for the tail, and threepence for the top, and if someone wanted a middle cut, tuppence. That's all. It was hard graft, but you didn't notice it, until you went into the services, then your holiday started. On a Sunday morning I got sixpence for doing some white washing.

I remember when our flare lamp wouldn't burn properly and I cleaned it with a thing called a pricker, and the dirt flew out with a 'phut' and so did a shower of paraffin, all over the fish, but we still sold it."

Chris Arnett

49   **W.Pink & Sons,** Pork Butchers

"I particularly remember the delicious pork sausages bought there at 8d a pound."

"Jim Bussy and his daughter ran the business and used to kill their own pigs in the back of the shop They used to queue up on a Saturday for his hot tripe."

"I had to learn to slaughter, prepare and dress carcases for the various meat departments. I also had to learn the cooked meat work and all its kindred arts. We used to bladder lard, roast legs of pork, salt and cook beef, and make pressed meats, saveloys, black puddings, chitterlings and of course pork and beef sausages. The faggots we made and put them in big baking trays which two of us lads humped down to a bakers shop further down Charlotte Street and when he had finished baking he would put our faggots into his oven to cook. We would collect them when done. They were delicious and sold very rapidly I can tell you."

51   **Mrs. Lamkin,** Fruiterer

"She was the Aunt of Joe Beckett the heavyweight boxer, I recall when Joe was going to have his crack at the world title (he was beaten by Georges Carpentier) he came to visit his Aunt. He lived in Southampton at the time, I think half the population gathered round the bottom of Charlotte Street to see him, somewhere around 1925 I think it was."

"After school they gave me a nice tea and I used to do different jobs for them such as cleaning the brass weights, cut up great big boxes of dates into ½lb and 1lbs ready for Saturday on the stalls, peel beetroot and get that ready. I used to enjoy myself at Lamkins."

53   **Charles Wingham,** Beer Retailer

The United Briton (1887-1948) a Biden's of Gosport house, later Portsmouth United Breweries.

55   **Mrs. Kitter,** Grocer

This was from 1925 to 1930 Steele's Fancy Goods.

"Fancy goods, toys and china shop, owned by Mr. Harry Steele, assisted by his wife, brother in-law Mr. Sid Hyams and Bessie, Mr. Steele's daughter. Early in 1925, at 14 I started work for Mr Steele and soon found him to be a very nice employer. On Saturdays it was stall day, outside his shop Mr H and I set it up and placed all the goods in position, dolls, half tea services, handbags, razor blades, "Bentima" pocket watches etc., and one empty tea chest bottom uppermost in a strategic position. Mr Hyams or Mr Steele would soon attract the customers with a few "free gifts" and then start. "This would cost £5 in any shop, £4, £3? O.K. it's my birthday today, have it for 21/-". Then down would come a tea service, same routine but with the frequent taking of a plate and banging it on the tea chest with a loud thump. These went for 7/6d or 10/-, a milk jug thrown in. Quite a brisk trade was done and I was hard pressed wrapping up those tea sets with so many "birthdays" that day. Periodically our van with the stall on top and packed with goods would set off for the fair on Portsdown Hill. The idea was a lucky number, with customers buying a numbered postcard for 6d each, the lucky winner picking one of the nice prizes. Another favourite sell was the "Flying Bird" large crates of these were bought. Each bird was made of paper-mache and from its body protruded a loose swallow tail. The whole was fastened to a stick by means of a thread and when held in the breeze, the tail whizzed around with a good whistle. Lots of these had to be threaded and Mr Hyams and I retired to the stall for a quiet couple of hours, helped along by tea brought along by Bessie or Mr Steele. They were of Jewish faith which made no difference to me, but a finer group of people I have yet to meet."

57   **Edward Passells,** Greengrocer

59   **Mrs. May Moger,** Toy Dealer

"Was kept by two old ladies, sisters, as a youngster I wondered how they did any trade. I mean most businesses scraped a living, but these two never seemed to sell anything. At least I never saw anybody in the shop except around the 5th of November. They always had fireworks every year, this was the only thing in the shop, for years it was the same old things stuck in the window."

"I remember old mother Moger, she used to chase us around the corner. She used to stand outside her shop like a toy soldier, she

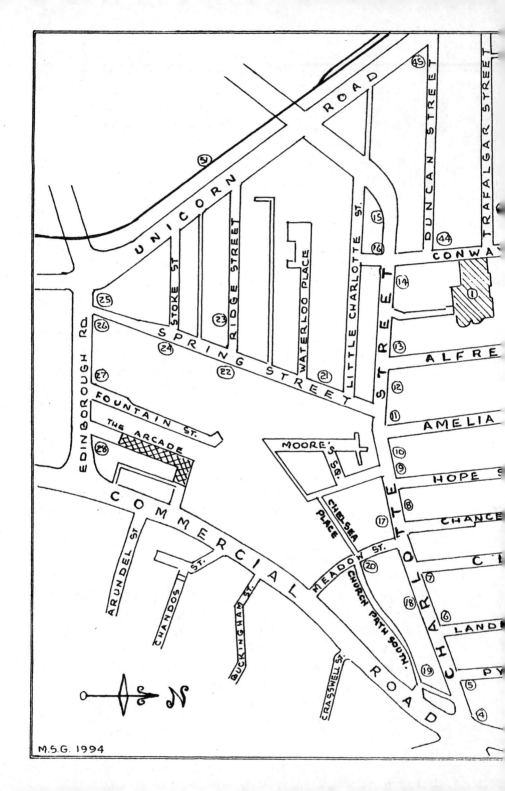

ABERCROMBIE ST.
COPENHAGEN STREET
TREET
NEW ROW
CHALTON ST.
FLATHOUSE ROAD
MARTHA ST.
THOMAS STREET
ENCE
STREET
SUSSEX PLACE
FREDERICK STREET
VICAR ROW
VIEW
47
49
48
42
35
41
40
34
33
39
32
38
31
37
3
36
50
30
29

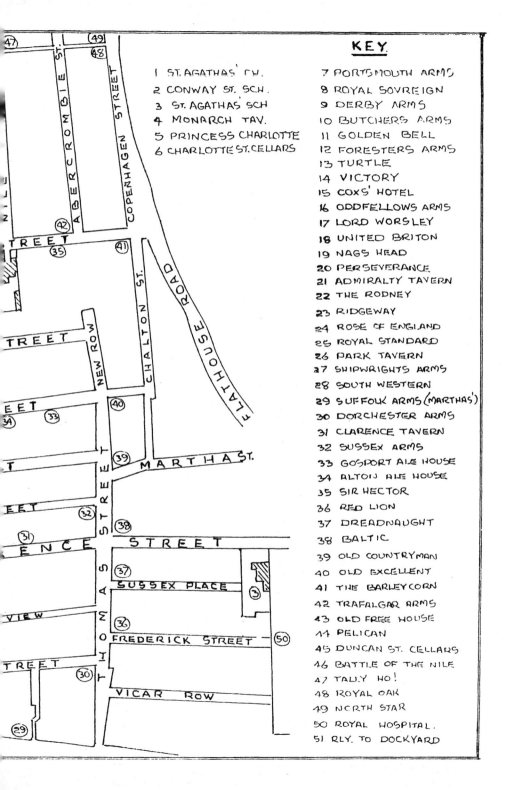

KEY.

1 ST. AGATHAS' CH.
2 CONWAY ST. SCH.
3 ST. AGATHAS' SCH
4 MONARCH TAV.
5 PRINCESS CHARLOTTE
6 CHARLOTTE ST. CELLARS
7 PORTSMOUTH ARMS
8 ROYAL SOVREIGN
9 DERBY ARMS
10 BUTCHERS ARMS
11 GOLDEN BELL
12 FORESTERS ARMS
13 TURTLE
14 VICTORY
15 COXS' HOTEL
16 ODDFELLOWS ARMS
17 LORD WORSLEY
18 UNITED BRITON
19 NAGS HEAD
20 PERSEVERANCE
21 ADMIRALTY TAVERN
22 THE RODNEY
23 RIDGEWAY
24 ROSE OF ENGLAND
25 ROYAL STANDARD
26 PARK TAVERN
27 SHIPWRIGHTS ARMS
28 SOUTH WESTERN
29 SUFFOLK ARMS (MARTHAS')
30 DORCHESTER ARMS
31 CLARENCE TAVERN
32 SUSSEX ARMS
33 GOSPORT ALE HOUSE
34 ALTON ALE HOUSE
35 SIR HECTOR
36 RED LION
37 DREADNAUGHT
38 BALTIC
39 OLD COUNTRYMAN
40 OLD EXCELLENT
41 THE BARLEYCORN
42 TRAFALGAR ARMS
43 OLD FREE HOUSE
44 PELICAN
45 DUNCAN ST. CELLARS
46 BATTLE OF THE NILE
47 TALLY HO!
48 ROYAL OAK
49 NORTH STAR
50 ROYAL HOSPITAL.
51 RLY. TO DOCKYARD

sold tiny wooden kiddies toys, wooden soldiers, little dolls prams etc."

Here is Meadow Street, named after the Mayor's Meadow which was earlier in this area of Landport. There as an alleyway right through from Commercial Road to Meadow Street, they used to call it Rats Lane and there were rats down there believe me. It was one of the quick ways to get to the Dockyard when Charlotte Street was full of stalls. The alley started in Lake Road by Drummond Road and continued on across Meadow Street to Moores Square and onto Spring Street.

61	**Arthur Dunsford,** Drug Store

"The German chemist on the corner of Meadow Street was interned all though the 1914 war."

63	**Frederick Wareham,** Butcher
65	**Robert Dyke,** Watchmaker
67	**Mrs. Ellen August,** Newsagent

"They used to sell American comics outside at a penny each."

69	**Charles Leach,** Confectioner

"Old Jacks"

"Leach's used to make herbal sweets."

"Outside Jacks looking in the window we could see peanut jelly, coconut ice, long sticks of rock, mint humbugs all made on the premises. We used to stand outside and smell it."

"A family business they made their own sweets at the rear of the shop, you could smell the boiling sugar with perhaps peardrops and essences of different flavours which they were making. Raspberry, blackcurrant, mint, lime and lemon were the main smells. They made all kinds of shapes, sticks of rock, Charlie Chaplin canes, door knockers etc. In the football season I remember men and boys selling Jacks famous "Cough No More" herbal sweets with aniseed, liquorice and paregoric. You could buy bags of odds and ends or mixed bags, mostly 6d to 8d a pound."

71	**Harry Rose,** Florist
73	**Henry Evans,** Newsagent

Later William Bryant, Newsagent

Charlotte Street

75　　**James Bryant,** Beer Retailer
The Lord Wolsley (1880-1934). Later after the war and rebuilding , Franks the newsagents were here.
"He started off selling from the back of a lorry in the traditional market style, later he moved into the shop."

77　　**Mrs. A Rowe,** Grocer
"What a shop that was. You could go in there and get anything, a pennyworth of jam in a cup, or treacle or sugar, a sawdust place but very nice good people."

Here is Moores Square. Possibly named after a former Mayor John Moore.

"When I left school my first job was at a pickle factory. Them days it was down Lancaster Road, Southsea. I had to wash dirty jars and bottles - believe me sometimes they were disgusting but the job had to be done. After we done that we had to peel onions and chop red cabbage. The work was hard and if you weren't careful you would cut your fingers and didn't they sting when you touched the vinegar. After a while the factory moved to Moores Square back of where Woolworths was.
When we had to start early I had to walk but mostly run around the walls by the Unicorn Gate to get there by 7 o'clock. I was frightened as there was a lot of Naval men going back to their ships or barracks. When I was on overtime I used to get 1½ times an hour extra. Sometimes I was lucky if I took home 7/6d a week to my mother. I gave her my money and had 1/- a week to myself. 6d of that was for my clothes club. One day at the factory I was walking past the outside stairs, I had a bucket of water put on me. I was drenched, I ran to my grandmother's and she dressed me with a pair of her drawers with buttons on the side, a long petticoat miles too big and a huge skirt and jumper. What a sight I was! I had to go home like it, everyone laughed. I'll never forget it. Once I was sent with a van to deliver the pickles it was hard working carrying the jars in and out of shops. When I went home for dinner I had the table to myself almost - I smelt of onions. I worked for Mr Foggarty. Happy Days."

　　　　　　　　　　　　　　　　　　　N.E Forysth

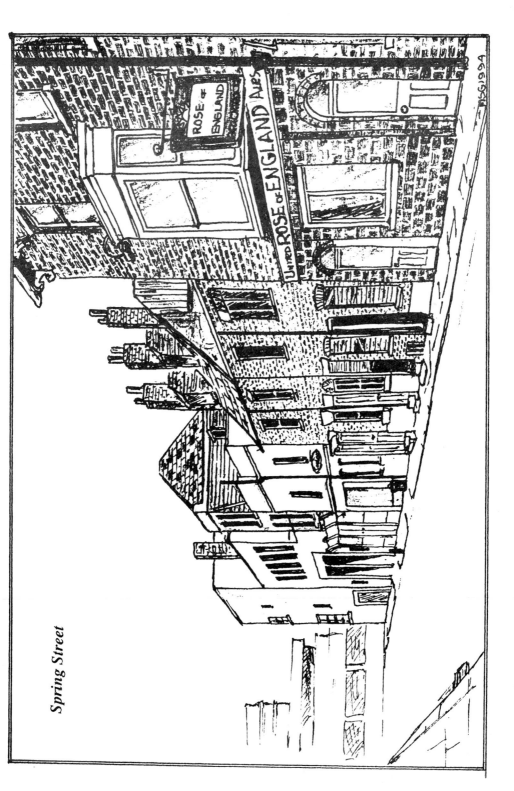

Spring Street

"One of my earliest recollections of Charlotte Street was going round to Moores Square as a youngster and going to a slaughter house, which I think was Harris' and seeing a bullock pole-axed. One wouldn't think that things went on down there like that, but that's precisely what consistently happened round the back of Marks and Spencers."

"A few houses down there and at the bottom a slaughter house. We did know the man who used to work there, Mr. Dagnell, he had one arm and used to swing one of those big picks with a spike on the end. He would hit the same spot every time right in the corner where the two horns came out. He was marvellous right in the middle every time."

79   **George Harris,** Butcher

"Harris the meat shop opposite Georges leather shop had a slaughter house in Moores Square. One day a cow escaped and charged into Georges, trouble was they could not turn the animal round, hence they had to back it out. I guess you could say the cow came looking for its hide."

81   **Alfred Webb,** Fruiterer

83   **James Smith & Sons,** Confectioners

"Lovely shop, always a nice show. They used to collect money all year round for Christmas, you would give them a bob or two when you could afford it."

85   **William Bates,** Baby Linen Dealer

87   **Mrs. Jones,** Greengrocer

89A   **William Valler,** Baker

here is Spring Street, so named because of the springs in the area which used to feed into the creek which later became the Millpond. It is now part of the Cascades Centre.

89-91   **The Alfred Arms**

Listed in 1863. The site was rebuilt as 1-4 Market Buildings.

         1-2   **Herbert Polman,** Leather Seller

         3   **Robert Negus,** Draper

             "Nothing over 2d, ribbons, pins, combs, etc."

         4   **Mrs. Elizabeth Negus,** Shopkeeper

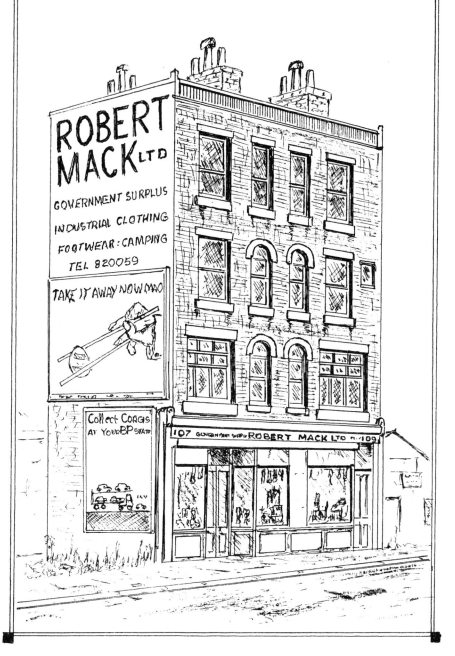

93	**Walter Houghton,** Bootmaker
95	**Peter Cotrell,** Tailor

"I remember Peter Cotrell, Navy Tailor, he used to take us around the streets on voting day on his cart. In the middle of the cart was a big dummy all dressed in Navy Whites. Everyone knew Cotrell and all the kids loved him, he was a well known character in Charlotte Street."

"Was well known in the Dockyard and delivered by donkey cart. The donkey was known to visit the Crown for his pint of beer. The ratings made a fuss of him, and his walk was a little unsteady when leaving the pub."

101   **James Gover,** Ironmonger.

The Govers took over from Hudsons. Later they moved to Meadow Street but closed when the Cascades Centre was built.

103-105   **C Duffy & Sons,** Confectioners

"Double fronted shop, both sides full of sweets, a beautiful shop."

107   **Robert Mack,** Army and Naval Stores

"Macks as it is popularly called has been another of the well known names in Charlotte Street. The family of Macks not only serving its customers in the market, but also serving the City by being members of Portsmouth Corporation. Dealing mainly in ex-government surplus and housed in a building that survived Hitler's blitzes, it is a four storey building, part Georgian and early Victorian edifice. The original deeds are said to be dated 1790. Restoration was carried out in 1952. The building gives some idea of what Charlotte Street looked like, with other premises built of the same type of brick and having similar windows. Unfortunately it has now been demolished with a lot of other buildings in the area to make way for the Cascades Shopping Centre.

"The original shop was just inside Meadow Street, on the corner of Moores Square. They came from Leeds in Yorkshire and his wife told me that her family were a Polish Jews and that her family name was Robinson, which ties up with the fact that a lot of Scotsmen went to jobs in Poland and Russia years ago."

109	**The West Riding Wallpaper Co. Ltd.**
111	**Mrs. Catherine Jones,** General Dealer

113	**Mrs. Constance Morris,** Tobacconist
115	**John Hart,** Butcher
117	**Harold Groves,** Tool Merchant
119	**Frederick Carter,** Shopkeeper
121	**Charlie Ward,** Shopkeeper
123	**James Penfound,** Florist

here is Conway Street

On the corner was the Welcome Mission

125-127 **The Hat Box,** Milliners

From 1863 to 1923 it was the Oddfellows Arms a Bransbury's house.

"Miss Edith Kinch had a lovely little shop, the windows dressed beautifully with summer hats, straw hats from Italy and Hungary and also Panama hats for ladies and children. Edith would teach a couple of girls or young women to decorate the plain straw hats with ribbons, flowers, feathers or little ornaments, you could buy a shape you fancied and she would dress it up for you. She also made brides headdresses. The trade was keen and competitive and for 3/11d you could have a most creative experience. Now and again she would have a sale and knock down prices. The winter stock came in from warehouses in London, felts and velours in bright colours to cheer up the long winter days."

here is Little Charlotte Street now part of the Cascades Centre.

| 129 | **Ranjit Signa,** Medical Herbalist |
| 129 | **Rd Keech,** Naval outfitter |

here is Unicorn Road named after the Unicorn Gate.

"There was a market for all kinds of ironwork mostly. I can only remember vaguely as we did not hang about when shopping with mother at the markets. What I do remember was loads of rusty nuts and bolts, pulley wheels, brackets, bits of chain, cast iron grills and trivets for fire places. Also tins of ex-government paint mostly battleship grey or Brunswick green. Sometimes there were large rusty trowels and coils of rope, tarred rope and thick rope for clothes lines. I hated that part of the market but the men would grovel about in it and the traders made a living."

Returning on the north side

100	**Edward Smith,** Furniture Dealer
94A	**Ronald Hughes Jnr,** Antique Furniture Dealer
94	**George Murphy,** China Dealer

here is Portsea View

| 92 | **George Henwood,** Tailor |
| 90A | **Frederick Walters,** Refreshment Rooms |

here is Conway Street named after Mr Conway

> "One side had streets leading out into Unicorn Road, they were all named after Nelson's battles. All these streets had cellars although they were flat fronted. In Conway Street was Conway Street School, which seems strange, St. Agatha's Church was close but St. Agatha's School was right down at Clarence Street."

90	**Frederick Whitaker,** Hairdresser
88	**Frederick Whitaker,** Milliner
84	**Willie Roe,** Fried Fish Shop
80-82	**Henry Hewitt,** Beer Retailer

Listed as The Victory from 1863 to 1887 and Victory Inn until 1964 it was a Brickwood's house.

St. Agatha's Church

Rebuilt in 1894 at a cost of £11,000 by William Light. The murals were added later by Heywood Sumner. The church was never completed as the north aisle was never added. Although the church survived the war the parish was bombed flat and in 1954 the last service was held. The building was then used as a naval store. The Lady Chapel was demolished in 1974 to make way for Market Way. The building has recently been renovated by the County Council and will open occasionally for exhibitions.

| 78 | **Mrs. Hancock,** Tobacconist |
| 74-76 | **Herbert Bell,** Fishmonger |

"He used to auction off the leftover fish at the end of the day."
"On the corner of Alfred Street were two fish shops, one was Bells, who also had one the other end and the other was Howarths. All my

Oddfellows Arms

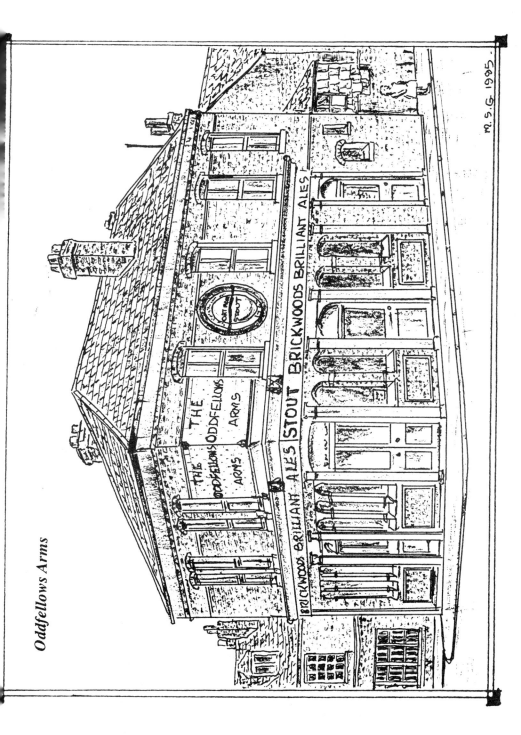

relations worked for Bells. He used to have his maid spy on them, sacked them one day and ask them why they didn't turn up for work the next. They had to work very hard, sometimes with their wages he would go round to the Chocolate King and buy them a bag of sweets or chocolate."

"I saw a girl and took a long time to buck up courage to speak to her, but spoke to Gladys Howard, the present Lady Mayoress (1986) serving in Bells"

here is Alfred Street named after Prince Alfred.

72	**James Howarth,** Fried Fish Shop	
70	**Abraham Levy,** Tailor	
68	**Mrs C Deacon,** Florist	
66	**Dittman & Malpas,** Corn Merchants	

"This was a shop that sold all kinds of pet food mostly for cats and dogs We did not like this shop much as they had hutches outside in the street with little puppies and kittens shivering with cold and fright. Another time there were canaries, song birds and pigeons for sale Chickens all fluffy and yellow when Easter came We used to ask for a pet but mum wouldn't let us have any, but we did have a pair of pigeons. They also sold mice and rats, straw, hay, baskets and bird cages. There was one irate parrot as well that would screech and call sometimes it talked. "Hello Jack" and then it would screech again."

64-66   Was the Foresters Arms from 1863 until 1891 a Young's house

62   **Arthur Robinson,** Trimming Merchant
Was from 1902 to 1932 Henry Kelloway the pawnbroker

60   **George Cooke,** Beer Retailer
The Golden Bell from 1863 until 1976. It had its own brewery until 1880 run by the Bailey family. Later it was run by H Mansbridge.
"On the corner of Amelia Street was the Golden Bell, there was lots of fights there, they used to fight over prostitutes. I've seen chairs come out of there."
"The landlord of the Golden Bell, Mr Harris, entertained his clientele, on the piano, which he played with great expertise, even to the extent of drawing the attention of passers by, who would stand and enjoy the free entertainment."

"I remember being taken to the Golden Bell in Charlotte Street. It was a small friendly, noisy bar, well I was small so the bar must have been small. It was mostly market traders. It was lovely, a gorgeous atmosphere well it appealed to me. We didn't stay there all evening, but it was a great place to visit on Saturday nights. I think it reminded me of London that's why I liked it."

"Outside the Golden Bell during the war there was a static water tank, a round one with wire mesh. On a bitterly cold Sunday lunchtime there was a bit of a shindy, apparently one person had bet another that he wouldn't get in the tank, which he did with all his clothes on. Well he won his bet, which was a pound, which was a lot of money in those days. To me it was always a bit of a rough dive on Saturday nights, with sailors there was always fights there. Not as though I drank as a boy, but it was a place to be avoided. The pickets were always there, I don't know about friendly."

here is Amelia Street, named after Princess Amelia.

"On one side of Amelia Street the houses had forecourts, gardens and cellars and were quite large houses for the area. Opposite were similar but smaller, flat fronted houses and at the Charlotte Street end was a much used Mission Hall, Zion Congregational Hall, I think. On Sunday it was used as a Sunday School, and during the week organisations used it. One in particular was the Band of Hope on Tuesday evenings. This meeting was always presided over by Mr Todd. I recall he used to drink water continuously though the meeting, as I grew older I wondered if he was drinking water. Also at the Charlotte Street end was J Cobb the hauliers who later moved to Spring Street after the bombing. The Street ran right through to Thomas Street where there was a Young's Brewery who employed a good percentage of the men in the area. Also here was the entrance to Chalton Street, where years previously temporary accommodation was especially built to house a party of Dockyard men from Scotland. This accommodation consisted of about twenty 2 roomed houses, where access to the upper floor was a ladder fixed to the wall. Toilet arrangements were shared with one W.C. and a cold tap, although each house had a gas ring installed"

T.E.Leyton & Sons in Amelia Street had trucks for hire and also built the market carts.

60B   **William Wakelin,** Confectioner
"He used to sell penny drinks. Vantas, a big globe, next to that an old gas bottle, they used to put a bit of gas in your drink."

58A-58B **Harold George,** Leather Seller
"Established in 1909 and closed in 1963 when Charlotte Street was rebuilt. A very sad day for those who had worked and lived in the street for so long."
"The dockyard men would crowd the leather shop out, buying leather etc., for mending the family footwear, almost a thing of the past now."
"I remember my dad used to come in with pieces of leather to mend our shoes, in those days he mended all our shoes. He would bring it in on his way home from the dockyard."

56-58   **James Malley,** General Merchant
Number 56 was the Royal Oak from 1863 to 1865, later in 1887 it was listed as the Butchers Arms, a Mew & Co. house.

54   **Charles Paine,** Greengrocer
52   **Frederick Crowson,** Fishmonger
50   **Charles Whipman,** Costumier
Was the Derby Arms from 1859 to 1891 a Burn's house, later a Brown's house.

here is Hope Street

William Tarring wrote of Hope Street "Then came a row of tiny houses with gardens in front of them, after a time another row of houses was built and the opening attained the title of Hope Street."

Later Don Tallack said "Although the style of houses varied they were all flat fronted. The brewery offices were situated on the corner of the Thomas Street end, next to the office the dray horses were stabled."

48   **Albert Griffiths,** Baker
46   **James Jones,** Oyster Bar
Was the Royal Sovereign from 1863 until 1891, originally a Long's house it became a Mew & Co. house.

"A well known business was Jones shellfish bar, cockles, mussels, lobster, crab, oysters of the finest quality. Oysters in my time were Bluepoints about 2/6d a dozen or Natives about 3/6d to 4/-, goodness knows what they are now. We used to pay 1/3d per pound for live lobsters."

"There was a cockle shop, where we used to buy a bag of whelks or cockles. Rose Jones was the daughter and if you bought something she would give you a little plate for nothing. When we bought whelks or cockles we would put lots of vinegar on them, take them to the pictures, tear the corner off the bag and drink the vinegar. Rose Jones later took over the pub in Spring Street which became the Rose of England."

44	**Mrs Helen Dunn,** Wardrobe Dealer
42	**Mrs E Deacon,** Florist
40	**Alfred Jordan (Exors Of),** Clothiers

This shop sold suits, coats, boots, etc. Heavy things.

here is Chance Street

"A very narrow street, you could almost shake hands with your neighbour across the street."

"I remember visiting a house in Chance Street, all the rooms were extremely tiny, two up, two down and no kitchen. The kettle used to be on a gas ring in the grate, if they had a cooker it was under a lean to at the back. When you went in the front door you stepped straight into the room, there was no passage."

38	**Alfred Jordan (Exors Of),** Clothiers

Executors of the estate were responsible for the business at this time. This shop dealt in underclothes, shirts etc., light things.

36	**F.L.Jeremy,** Wallpaper Merchant
36A	**Mrs Martha Jeram,** Greengrocer
32-34	**George Brooks,** Grocer

"I remember Mr Brooks' grocery shop in Charlotte Street, what a beaming happy face he had and nothing was too much trouble."

"They used to grind their own coffee, beautiful smell."

32	**Amelia Brooks,** Off Licence.

"Also on sale was Fremlins Elephant brand ale and oatmeal stout, 7/- per dozen pints."

here is Clarence Street

In which stood St. Agatha's Church School. This was built in 1812 as a Bell School at a cost of £1,200. It become All Saints Parish School but by 1859 was declared unfit for use. It was restored in 1899 by St Agatha's.

Also in Clarence Street was Clarence Street Baptist Chapel built in 1798, and rebuilt in 1839. When the Baptists transferred to Commercial Road it became St Agatha's Gymnasium.

> William Tarring mentions the chapel in his notes "My grandparents were very early members of the church there and I have often attended with the old lady the services there, she used to let me sit in the north Gallery. The people were well up in the congregation singing I have heard them render 'Vital Spark' and 'Sound the loud Timbrel' with good effect, but the ordinary singing was rather dreary.
> There was a "Three decker pulpit" with a clerk's desk below it. The clerk, old Mr. Bazill, a wooden legged dairyman who in a rather drawly tone said "let us sing to the praise and glory of God". He would proceed to give out a hymn two lines at a time which I thought since reminiscent of the Brick Lane tea party where they sang "The Jolly Young Waterman" to the same measure. There were galleries on each side that on the east being devoted to the string band and choir. For some cause or other they tired of their grand old chapel and built a much smaller one a brick semi-gothic creation in the Commercial Road *(in 1885)* leaving their Alma Mater to the Philistines led by Father Dolling who turned it into a gymnasium."

> "This street had two sections, Charlotte Street to Thomas Street and Thomas Street to Flathouse Road. There were flat fronted houses some with steps up to the front door. There were corner shops at the junction with Thomas Street. The second section housed the Royal Navy Swimming Baths. Also in Clarence Street was the drill hall belonging to St Agatha's Church. That hall was a treat for each class of the school, one half morning a week the class marched from the school to the hall for P.T. and games."

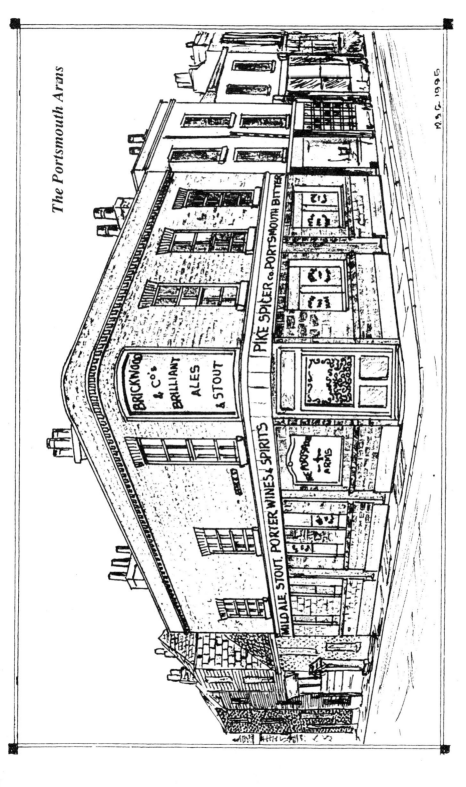

The Portsmouth Arms

30   **Portsmouth Arms, Arthur Smith**
1823 to 1964 was a Spicer's house.

28   **Misses P & B Kitter,** Costumiers
"Ladies nearly new shop."
"They used to hire out dressed for special occasions, you took them back the next day."

26   **Frank Toogood,** Hairdresser
"It was marked by the traditional red and white striped pole, rather a long one which came from ship, the bracket which held the pole spanned two shops, Toogood's and Kitter's next door. This pole eventually rotted away and was replaced with a flat board, also painted red and white. Painted on the window were the words Shaving and Hairdressing Saloon. The shop had a long bench inside, with a cushion stuffed with horsehair for his customers to sit on while awaiting their turn. Spittoons were also provided but often missed. In common with others they had their regular customers, one of these was a well known figure, sported a handlebar moustache."
"My father took me with him when he went for a short back and sides, when he was finished, it was my turn and a board placed across the arms of the chair for me to sit on. Some lads would go in for a ha'pe'th of hair oil which was applied there and then to slick their hair down."
"4d haircut, 3d shave - most barbers did shaving also moustache trimming and beard trimming after a haircut."

24   **Frederick French & Son,** Leather Merchants
22   **Abraham Isenberg,** Outfitter
"He made my wedding suit in 1946, blue herringbone. He didn't even measure me but it was a perfect fit.
"I remember Abraham Isenberg, he used to have two shops and he served in them both. We used to go in his shop and he would say "What do you boys want - caps?" and he would get out a big drawer and leave us to choose what we wanted whilst he went to his other shop. Then when we had chosen we would go over and pay for them. He would say "They look nice boys" when the only thing holding them up was our ears!"

20   **Frederick Saunders,** Beer Retailer

Charlotte Street Cellars from 1880 to 1964, a Young's house. Each Young's pub had a picture showing HMS Victory and HMS Renown. Motto Young's Victory Ales gain their Renown. The ales were Victory and the stouts Renown.

"There was old Fritz, he was a black man, who always dressed in black. He carried this little black case, I never saw what was in the case, I was too young, but he used to go around all the pubs selling things to sailors."

here is Landport View

16-18   **M Gaiman,** Grocer

Reasonable priced grocers, a penny or two cheaper than other grocers, with branches elsewhere in the town.

14   **A H Dart & Co.,** Printers

They later traded in Kingston Road

12   **Barker Biscuit Co.**

Was the Dorset Ale House from 1863 to 1865

10   **Daniel's,** Florist

Later Deacons.

here is Pye Street

"At the back of Pye Street were some stables, they belonged to E.G.Curtiss, seed merchants. Well, as a boy I used to watch these big horses leave the Dockyard where they worked, about twenty of them, big dray horses, and they would follow the leading horse to their stables, each horse knew his own stall and it was a marvellous sight."

"This street was cobble stones, the Dockyard horses were stabled here and there were also several slaughterhouse."

"I remember the almshouses, one up, one down."

Near here was St James Hall, a boxing ring and dance hall.

"The Ring was used by local boxers Stoker Bob Reynolds (middleweight), P.O. Frank Stubbs (heavyweight). It was also used for dancing, more of a local hop for the boys and girls, but no doubt togged up to the nines."

"Oh yes, I remember the Ring, not a very big place it cost 6d to get in. The boxers were Rob Goldring a local lad and Eric Gates from the Isle of Wight and somebody called fudge. It closed about 1936."

"After the Ring closed the bouts were transferred to the Connaught Drill Hall with various trainers, Jack Smith, Benny Clarke, Gus Tout etc. The boxers were Billy Streets, Len Lemoux, Kid Connor, Rob and Len Goldring, Matt George, George and Monty Brown and Jack Fiford to mention a few."

8   **D Davidson & Son,** Outfitters

From 1823 until 1865 the Eden Brewery was here, founded by Joseph Brown it was later run as a trust for his orphans and grandchildren. Brown & Co was run by various managers. The premises became a Bransbury's beer house by 1880 and in 1887 is listed as The Brewery Tap.

Quoting from William Tarring again "The brewery premises extended back to Pye Street in the rear thereof. The plot of ground extending from Pye Street to Landport View was a kind of stockyard on the back part of which stood a wooden erection which was used as a butcher's shop. I saw that house moved on wheels or rollers to the upper end of Pye Street where it was incorporated in the premises of Mr. H.Davis - Engineers."

"Ladies outfitter, he was very good to the poor, schools and gave coats to the poor"

"On Sunday mornings you could buy a new cap for 6½d and a new shirt for 1/6d."

"Dave Davidson, you could go in there and knock him down on the price of a dress, if he wanted £2 you could beat him down to £1."

"Joe Davidson was very good to the poor of the area, at Christmas time he always ran a party for the children of the area in the old St James Hall and we all came out afterwards with the usual orange, couple of apples and a bag of sweets. Later he became a councillor. On one of his successes in the local elections he celebrated by giving the poor children of Portsea clothes, dresses for the girls and trousers for the boys."

6	**Philips Bros. (Boots) Ltd.,** Boot Factors
4 .	**Sydney Roberts**, Linen Merchant
2	**The Monarch,** Charles Brown.

From 1863 until 1962 becoming The Crown from 1964 until 1976. The premises then became a jewellers and is now empty. It was originally a Brown's house, later Brickwoods with a brown glazed front.

> The spluttering Naphthalene lamps glowing white,
> The Roasting beef pieces hung up in full sight,
> The shopping crowds jostling to left and to right,
> In Charlotte Street market, on Saturday night.
>
> The crash of the boxes, the coster boys' cry,
> The scrawny grey chickens by vendors held high,
> The smell of the batter of fish on the fry,
> In Charlotte Street market, in times long gone by.
>
> Bananas and flowers, on green battens hung,
> The ladders with postcards pinned up on each rung,
> The cold meat stands offering pork pies and tongue,
> In Charlotte Street market, when we were so young.
>
> The paving stones dark with the rain of November,
> The hot chestnuts roasting in red glow of ember,
> The first Christmas trees that portended December,
> In Charlotte Street market - ah, do you remember?
>
> J.O.Woon

This booklet was compiled by the members of the W.E.A. Local History Group which meets at the New Road Adult Education Centre, Balliol Road, Buckland. The group is made up of local people who wish to record the history of ordinary peoples' lives and the streets in which they live. The group is very informal and welcomes new members who care to come to New Road on a Tuesday evening during term time or write to us.

Current Class Members:

> Leonard Bufton, Anton Cox, Frank Deacon, Peter Eaves, Betty Fowkes, Peter Galvin, Malcolm Garlick, Kevin Goldring, Pat Goldring, Charles Hutchins, Stephen Pomeroy (Chairman & Editor), Chris Redgrave, Jeff Smith, Rita Wall and Margaret Webster (Treasurer).

Honorary Members:

> Olive Cook (Proof reader), Don Miles (Typesetting)

Affiliated Members:

> Des Beaumont, Morecambe, Lancashire
> Vic Burly, Brisbane, Australia
> Maggie Munro, Frankstone, Australia

Contributors:

> Chris Arnett, Mrs E. Clark, Ruby Enright, Mr George Jnr., Kathy Heywood, N.E.Forsyth, Bill Hockley, Ivy Hunt, the late Harry Ingamills, Elsie King, E. Pratt, Mrs V.M. Priest, Dr. Lucy Slater, Rose Smith, Vera Sparkes, Mrs Stanley, Memories of John or William Tarring (Portsmouth City Record Office), Lilian Taylor, R. Toogood, Mr Wade, Norman Wayman, Tom Winsor and J.O. Woon.

Class Members in 1987:

> Bartholomew Albertolli, Len Bufton, Maud Dalley, Frank Ford, Peter Galvin, Charles Hutchins, George Linton, Dave Jenkins, Stephen Pomeroy, George Smith, Jeff Smith, Don Tallack and Margaret Webster.